RECORDED VERSIONS GUITAR

AUTHENTIC TRANSCRIPTIONS WITH NOTES AND TABLATURE

Transcribed by DAVE WHITEHILL

Stevie Ray Vaughan and Double trouble

The Sky is Crying

ISBN 0-7935-1555-6

Photos by John T. Comerford III

HAL•LEONARD CORPORATION

7777 W. BLUEMOUND RD. P.O. BOX 13819 MILWAUKEE, WI 53213

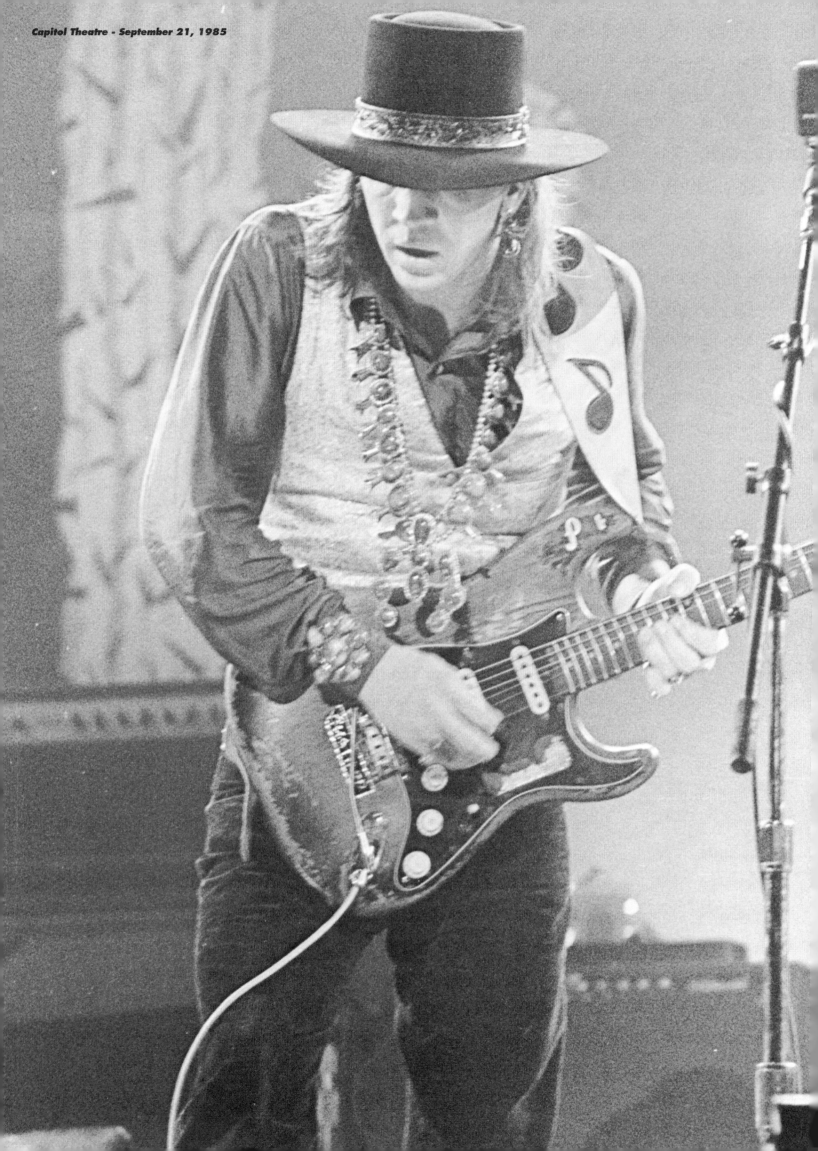

Boot Hill

Arranged and Adapted by Stevie Ray Vaughan

Tune down 1/2 step

Medium Blues Shuffle (♩. = 100)

Intro

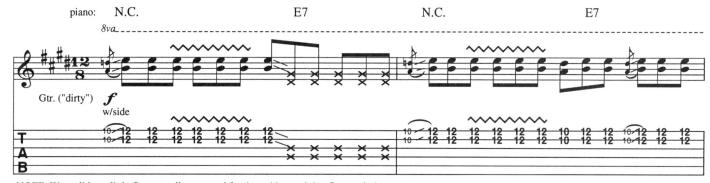

NOTE: Wear slide on little finger to allow normal fretting with remaining fingers during verse.

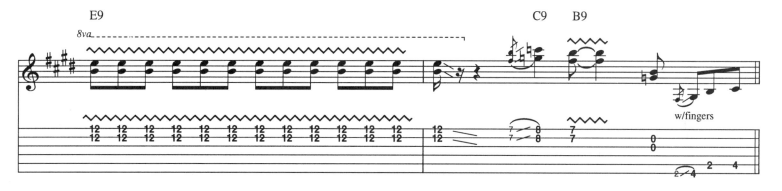

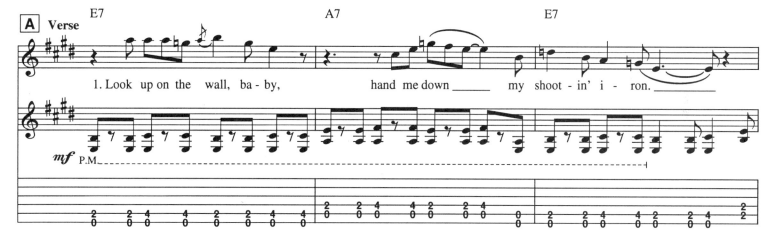

1. Look up on the wall, ba-by, hand me down ____ my shoot-in' i-ron. ____

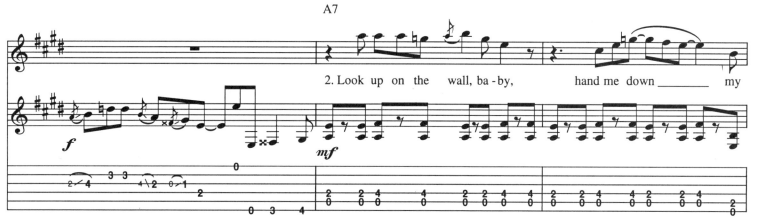

2. Look up on the wall, ba-by, hand me down ____ my

shoot - in' i - ron. _____

Call your moth - er long - dis-___ tance, tell her to ex - pect your bod - y

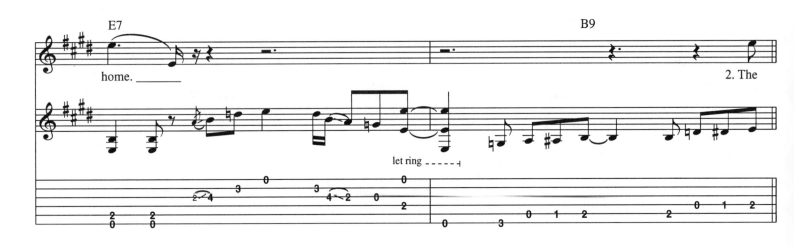

home. _____ 2. The

B Verse

sen - ate don't burn you, ba - by, Lord knows the coun -

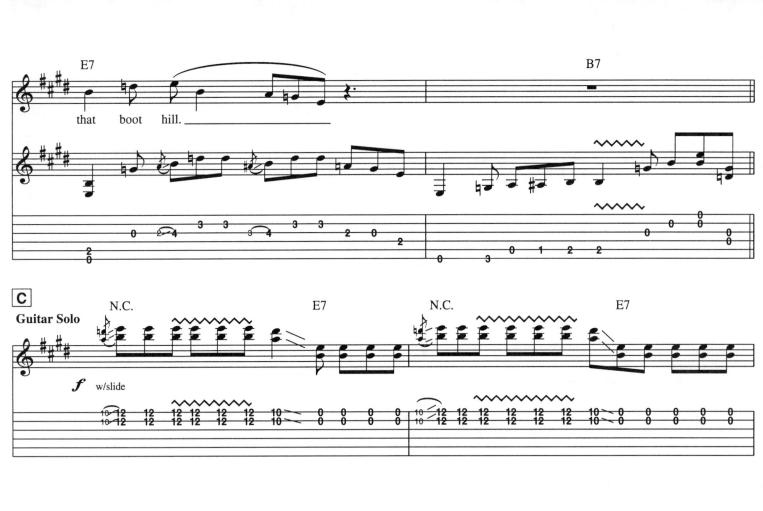

that boot hill. _____

C

Guitar Solo

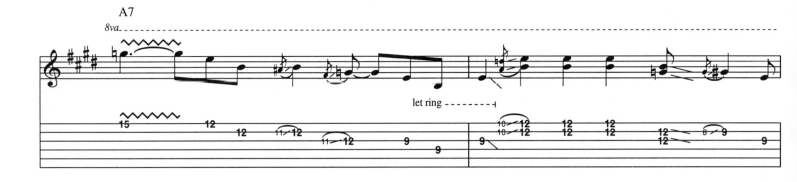

* Raise pitch by moving slide between 3rd and 4th frets.

D **Verse**

don't wan - na wax you dar - lin', 'cause you gave me my _____

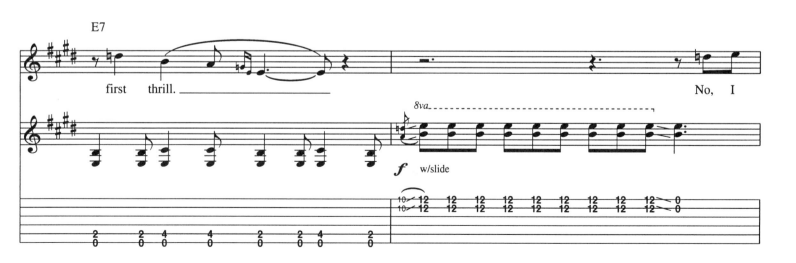

first thrill. _____ No, I

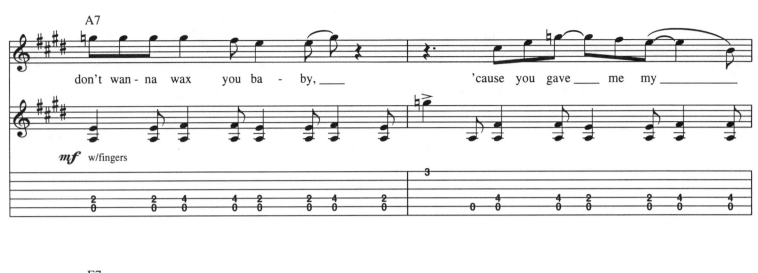

don't wan-na wax you ba - by, ____ 'cause you gave ____ me my ____

first thrill. ____ You

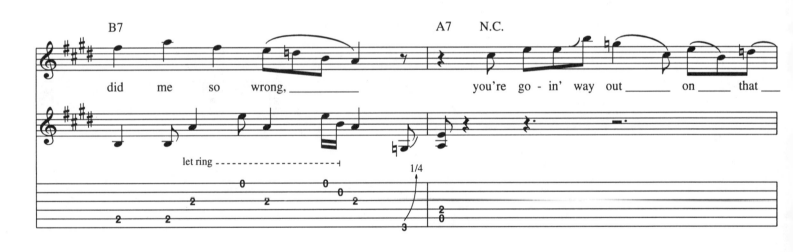

did me so wrong, ____ you're go-in' way out ____ on ____ that ____

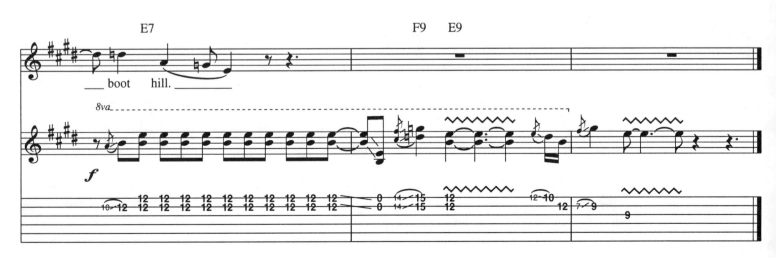

____ boot hill. ____

The Sky Is Crying

By Elmore James

Tune down 1/2 step

Slow Blues (♩. = 55)

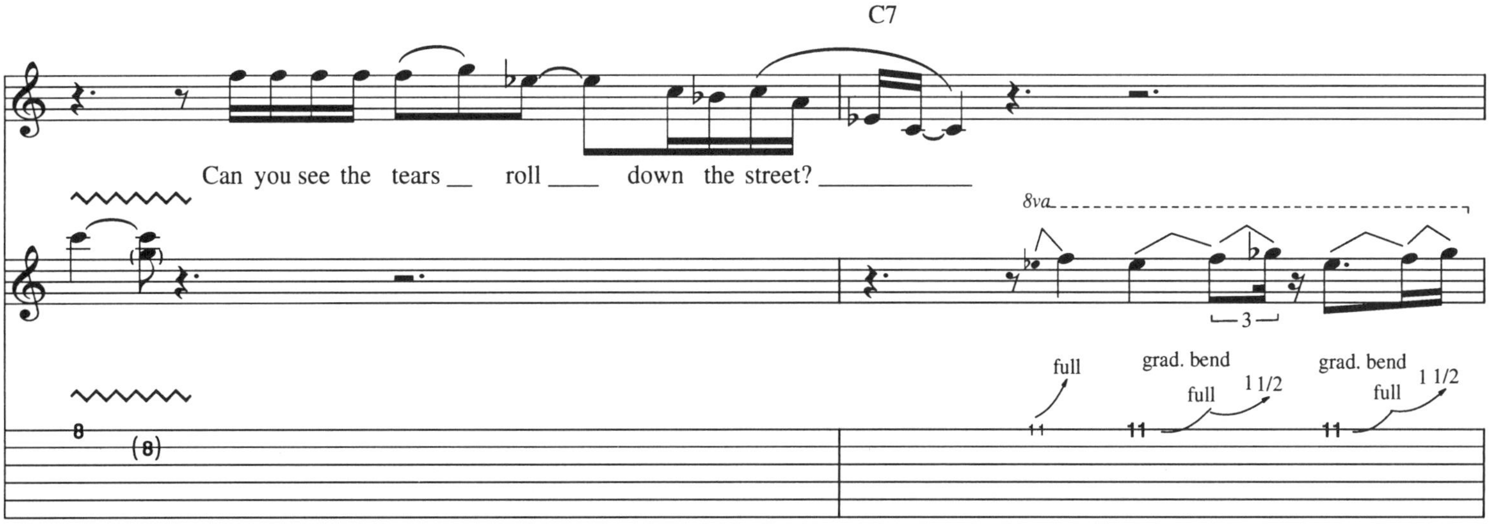

Count Basie Theater - June 26, 1985

Empty Arms

By Stevie Ray Vaughan

the day that I'm gone. _____

'Cause I'm leav-in' in the morn-in', won't ___ be back at all. _____

C Verse

2. You have run _____ me rag-ged, ba - by, 's your own fault __ you're on your
___ to get me back, ba - by, with all your tricks and charms, _

own. _____

You __ have __ run _____ me rag-ged, dar - lin',
You __ can__ try _____ to get me back, ba - by,

Little Wing

Words and Music by Jimi Hendrix

*High D note sounded by pressing down firmly
on the edge of a 21-fret neck ("imaginary 22nd fret").

**Switch pickup selector switch to bridge and then middle position.

NOTE: Finger vibrato inadvertently causes prebend on ③ to sound.

* ③ sounds at random throughout trill.

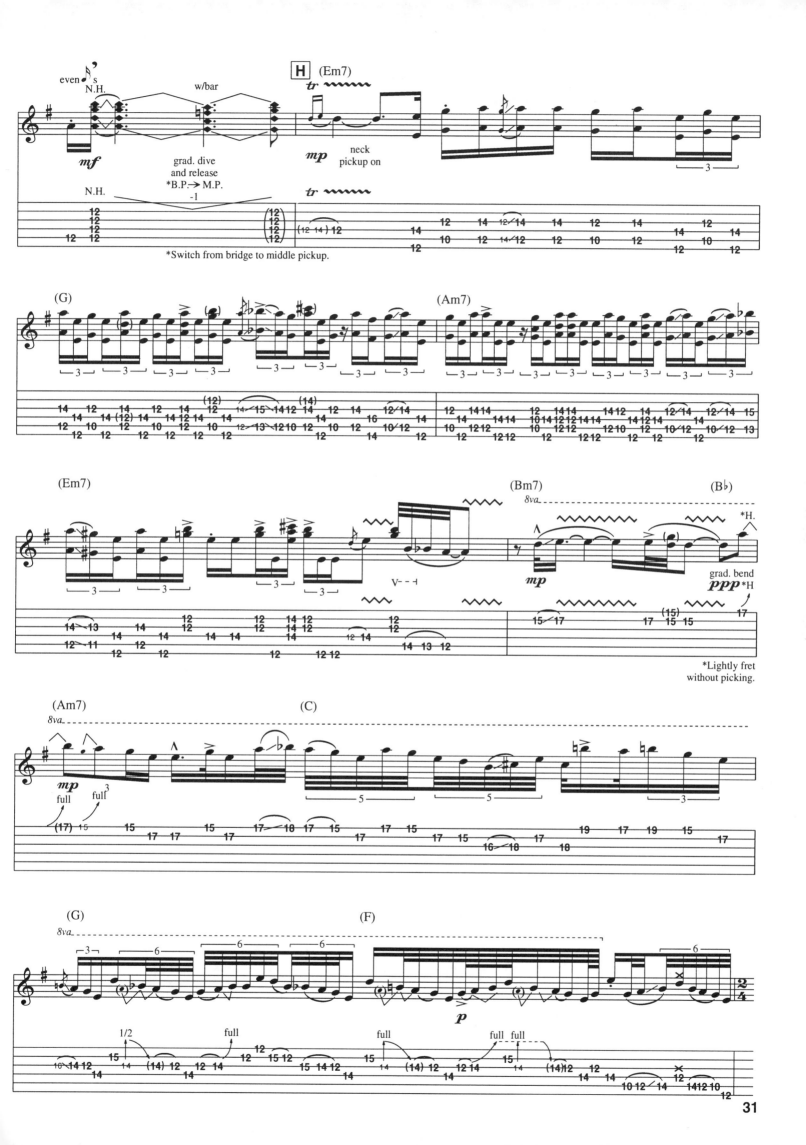

34

Count Basie Theater - June 26, 1985

Wham

By Lonnie Mack

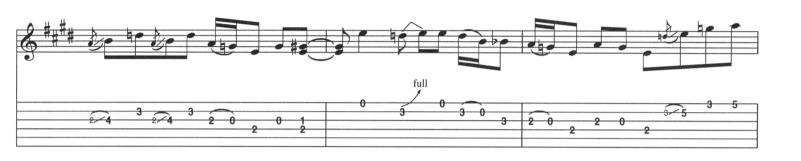

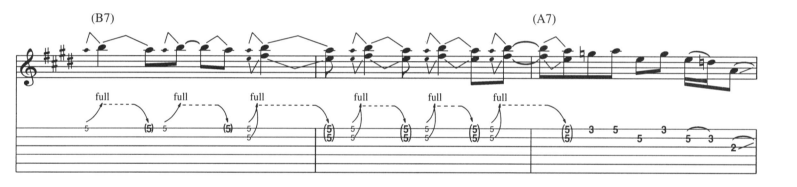

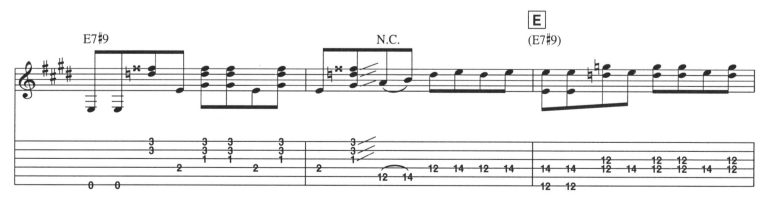

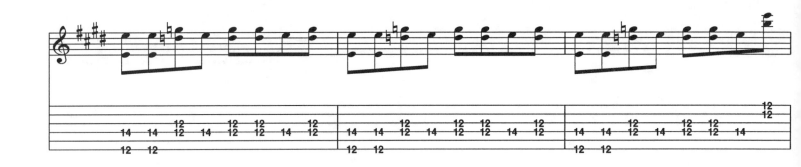

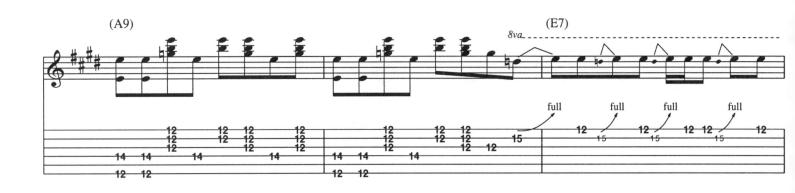

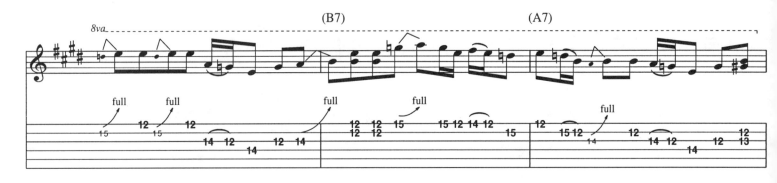

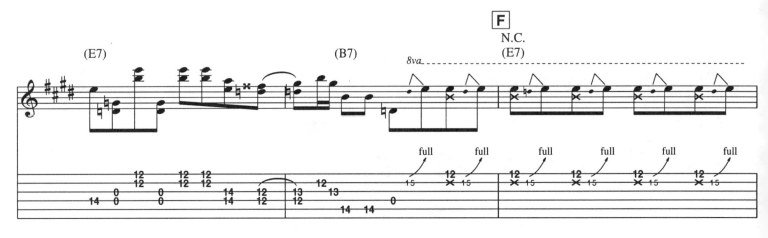

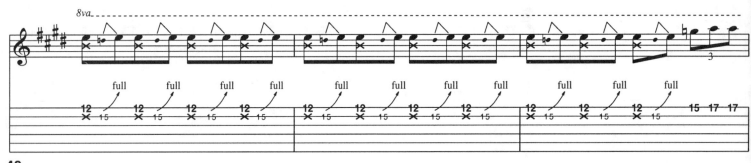

*Fret ⑥ w/thumb

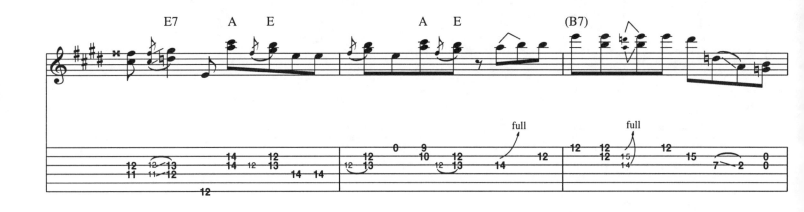

D.C. al Coda

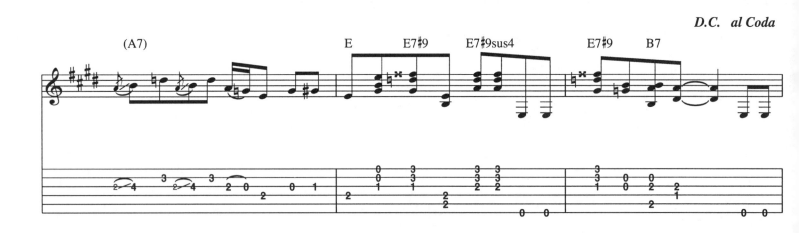

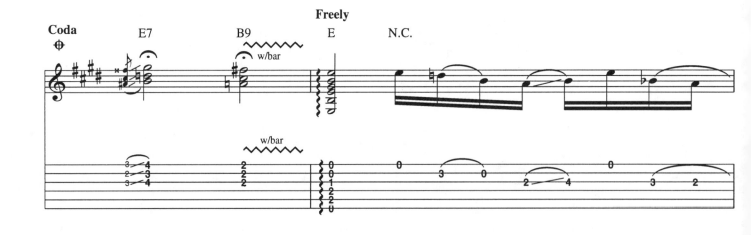

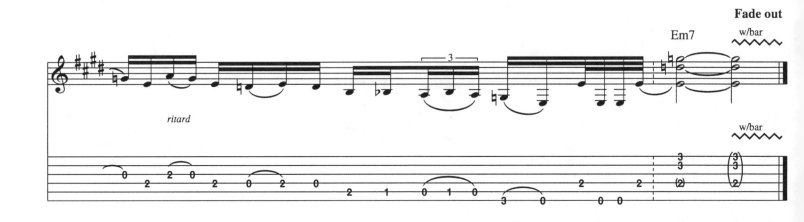

May I Have A Talk With You

By Chester Burnette

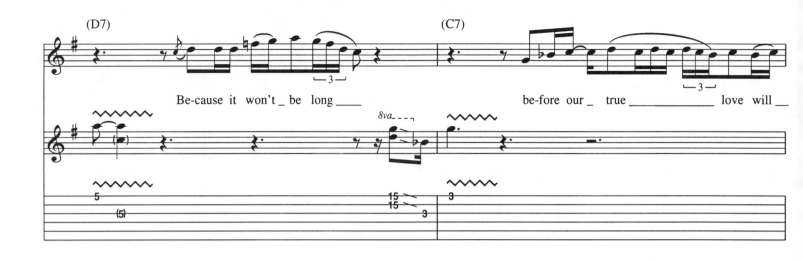

Be-cause it won't _ be long ____   be-fore our _ true _____ love will _

be through.

C Guitar Solo

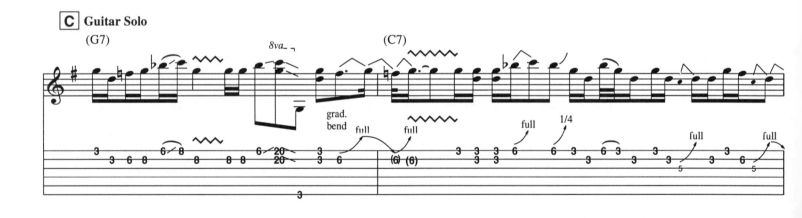

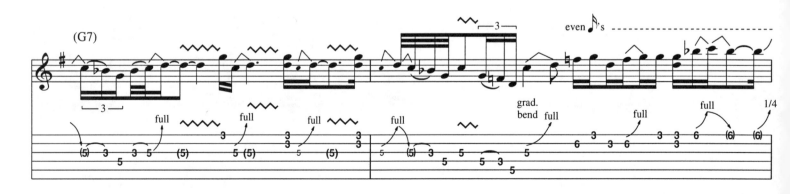

* Pull-off sounds ① & ②

48

3. You know I like my cof-fee sweet in the morn-in'

and I'm cra - zy 'bout my tea at night.

Yeah, I like ___ my cof-fee sweet in the morn-in', lit-tle girl,

and I'm cra - zy 'bout my tea at night.

You _ know you're com-in' a lit-tle bet-ter now, ba - by.

Freely

All I ___ want ya to do,   treat me right. _____

* Progression inferred by bass line

Count Basie Theater - June 26, 1985

Close To You

By Willie Dixon

Tune down 1/2 step

Intro

Lively Blues Shuffle (♩. = 120)

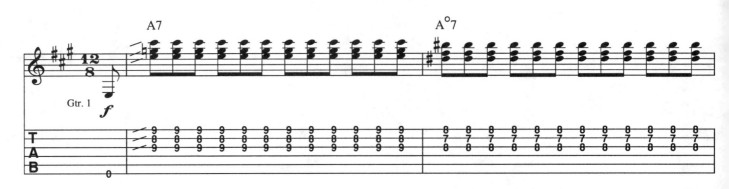

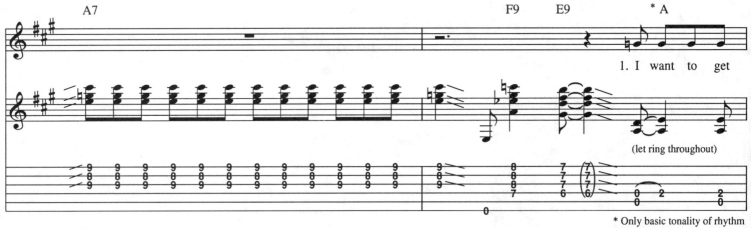

(let ring throughout)

1. I want to get

* Only basic tonality of rhythm figures will appear in harmonic analysis. All complete chords are named throughout.

close to you, ba - by, as a I can get.
close to you, ba - by, as a white is to rice.
close to you, ba - by, as the whites of your eyes.

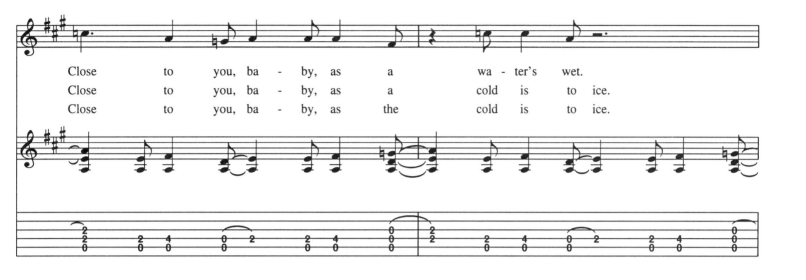

Close   to   you, ba - by,   as   a   wa - ter's   wet.
Close   to   you, ba - by,   as   a   cold   is   to   ice.
Close   to   you, ba - by,   as   the   cold   is   to   ice.

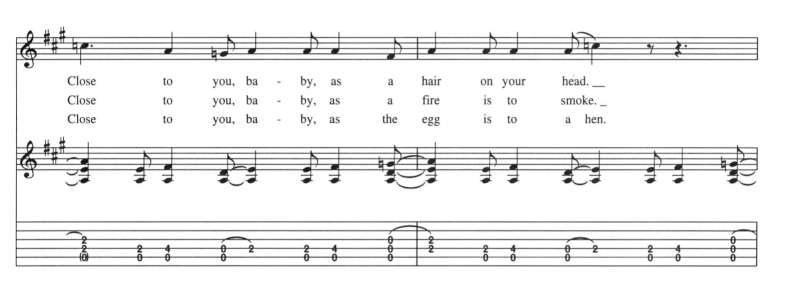

Close   to   you, ba - by,   as   a   hair   on your   head. __
Close   to   you, ba - by,   as   a   fire   is   to   smoke. __
Close   to   you, ba - by,   as   the   egg   is   to   a hen.

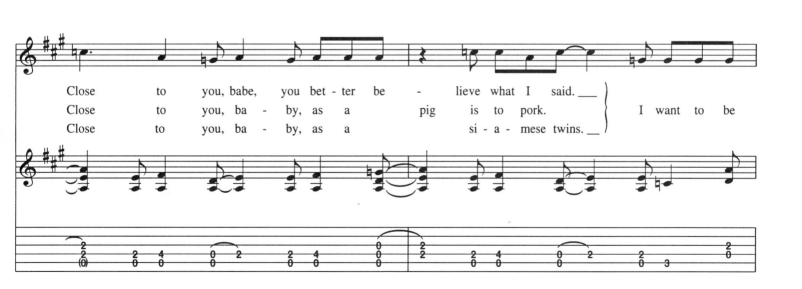

Close   to   you, babe,   you bet - ter be - lieve what I   said. ___
Close   to   you, ba - by,   as   a   pig   is   to   pork.   I want to be
Close   to   you, ba - by,   as   a   si - a - mese twins. __

Chorus

close _____ to you, ba - by.   Yeah, lit - tle bit

2nd time play Fill 1

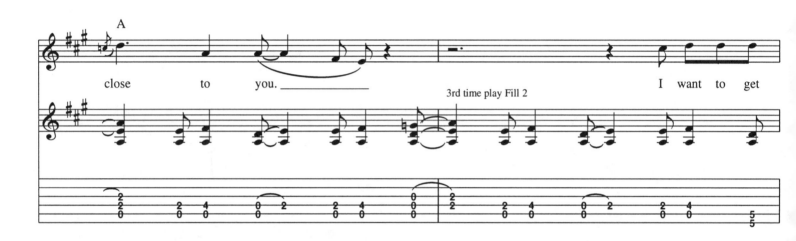

close   to   you. _____   I   want   to   get

3rd time play Fill 2

To Coda ⊕

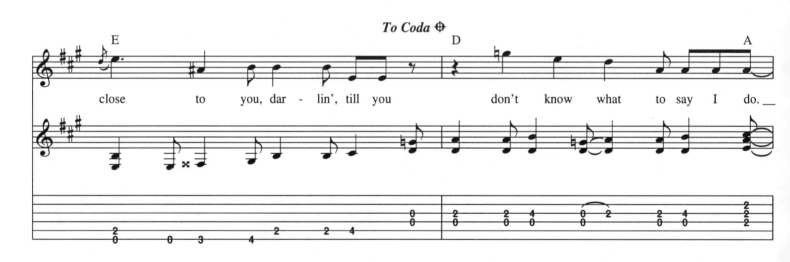

close   to   you, dar - lin', till you   don't know what   to say I do. __

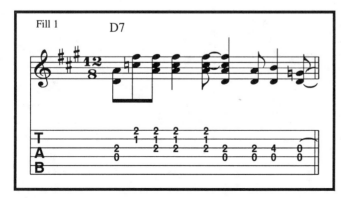

Fill 1   D7

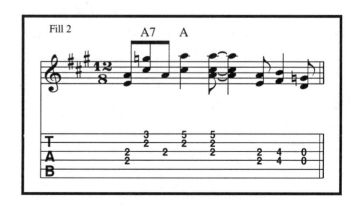

Fill 2   A7   A

* Unintentional note

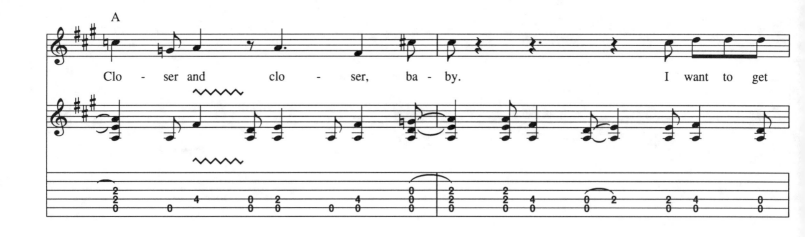

Clo - ser and clo - ser, ba - by. I want to get

To Coda ⊕

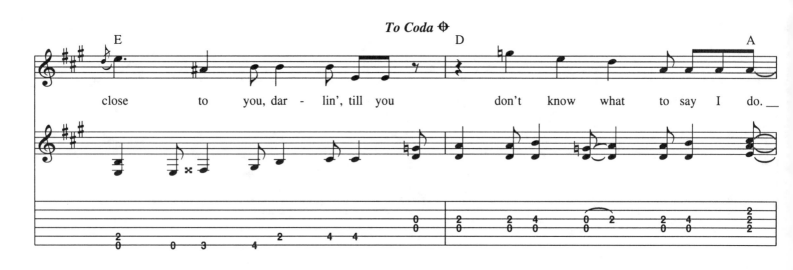

close to you, dar - lin', till you don't know what to say I do.

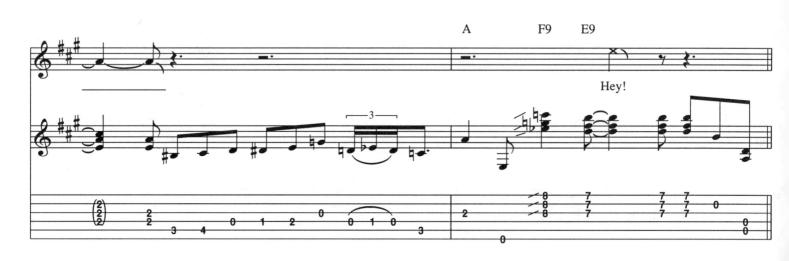

Hey!

D Guitar Solo

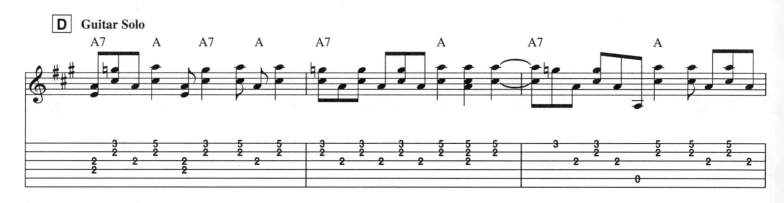

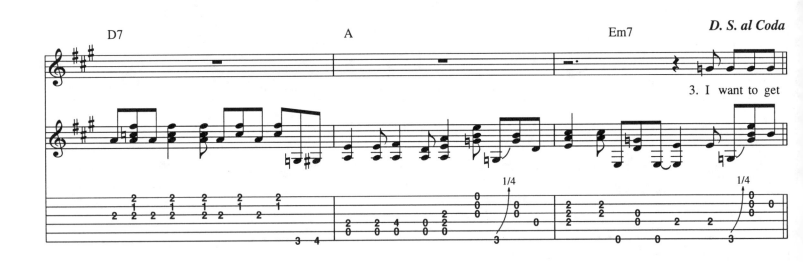

D. S. al Coda

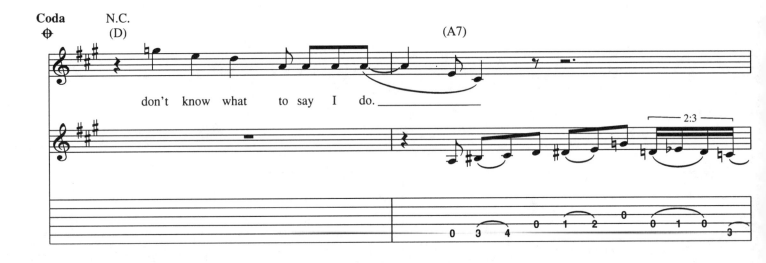

3. I want to get

don't know what to say I do. _____

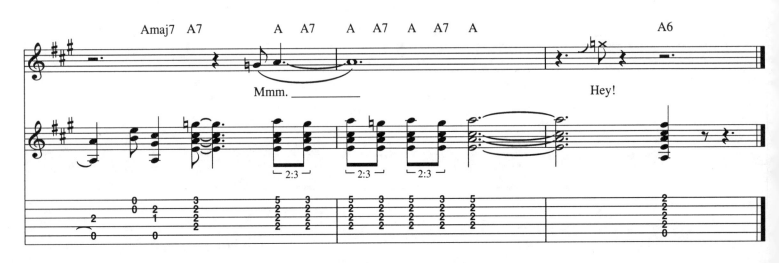

Mmm. _____

Hey!

Chitlins Con Carne

By Kenny Burrell

Note: Melody played in octaves á la Wes Montgomery throughout.
Use thumb strokes instead of pick except for soloing.

* Notes in parantheses
are all unintentional.

* Play slightly behind the beat.

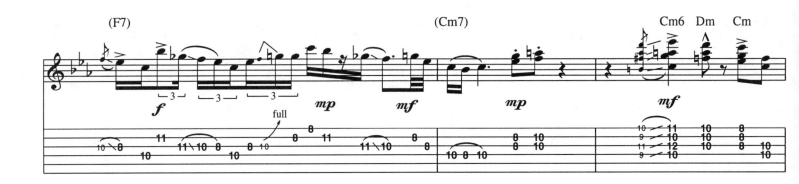

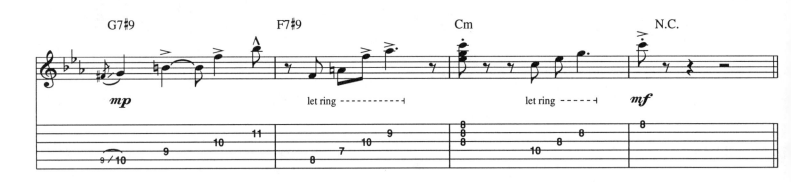

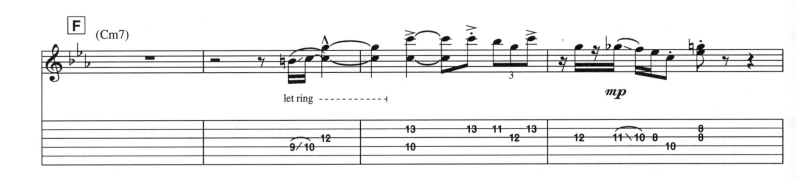

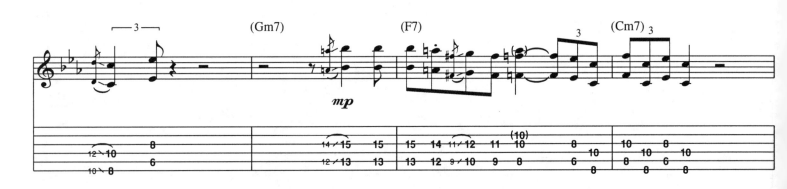

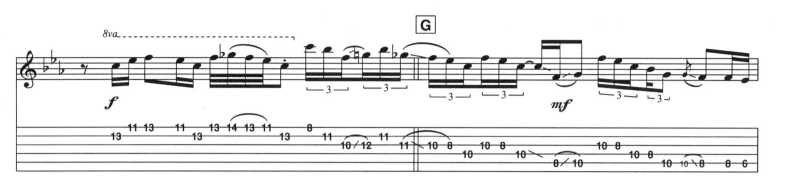

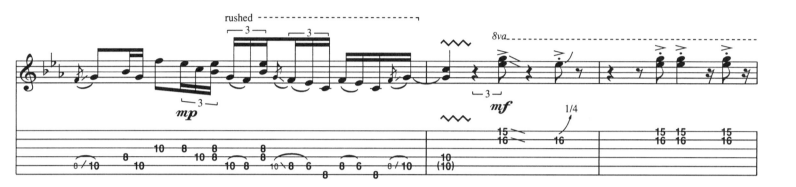

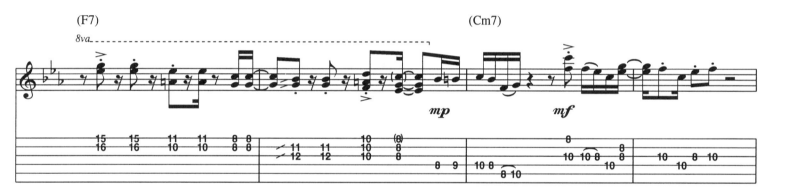

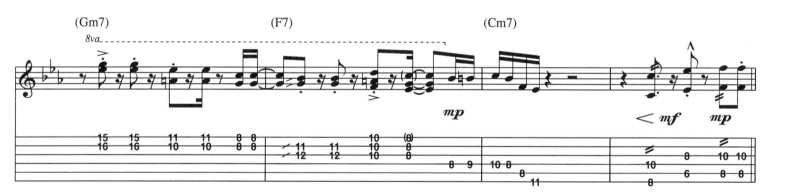

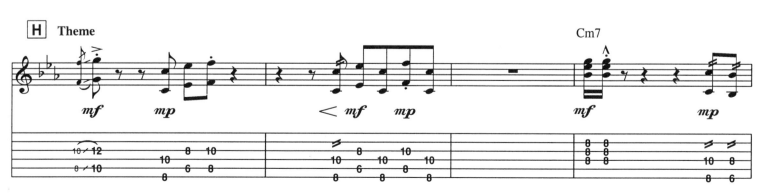

Utica, New York - January 23, 1986

So Excited

By Stevie Ray Vaughan

NOTE: Modal key signature of A Dorian is used here for ease in reading. However, although melodies are primarily minor (i. e. blues scale based), the bass lines infer dominant harmonies throughout. Suggested accompaniment appears in parantheses.

* partial
release

Life By The Drop

By Doyle Bramhall and Barbara Logan

Moderate Blues Shuffle (♩ = 98)

Swing Feel ♫ = ♩ ♪

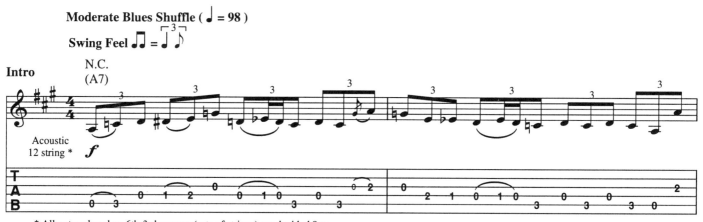

* All notes played on 6th-3rd courses (sets of strings) are doubled 8va.
Remaining courses are unisons. Unlike previous songs, this one is in
standard tuning.

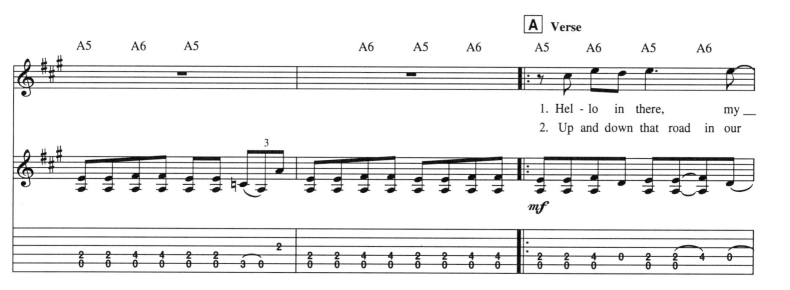

1. Hel - lo in there, my __ old __ friend. __
2. Up and down that road in our worn out shoes. __

Not so long a - go __ it was till the end.
Talk - in' 'bout good things and sing - in' the blues.

NOTATION LEGEND